This book belongs to

....

For Mary and Matthew,
my curious research companions

In Dust and Sandals
Copyright © 2022 by Deborah Paine
Published 5th November 2022

In Dust and Sandals

Written and Illustrated by **Deborah Paine**

In dust and sandals
we roam about,

up in the trees and down on the ground.

harvest what nature
gives us.

granaries filled
to plenitude.

Men and women
work the field

to plant and harvest
corn and wheat,

to feed animals,
for winter storage,

We knead dough
to make breads

Horses eat heartily
the hay they earn,

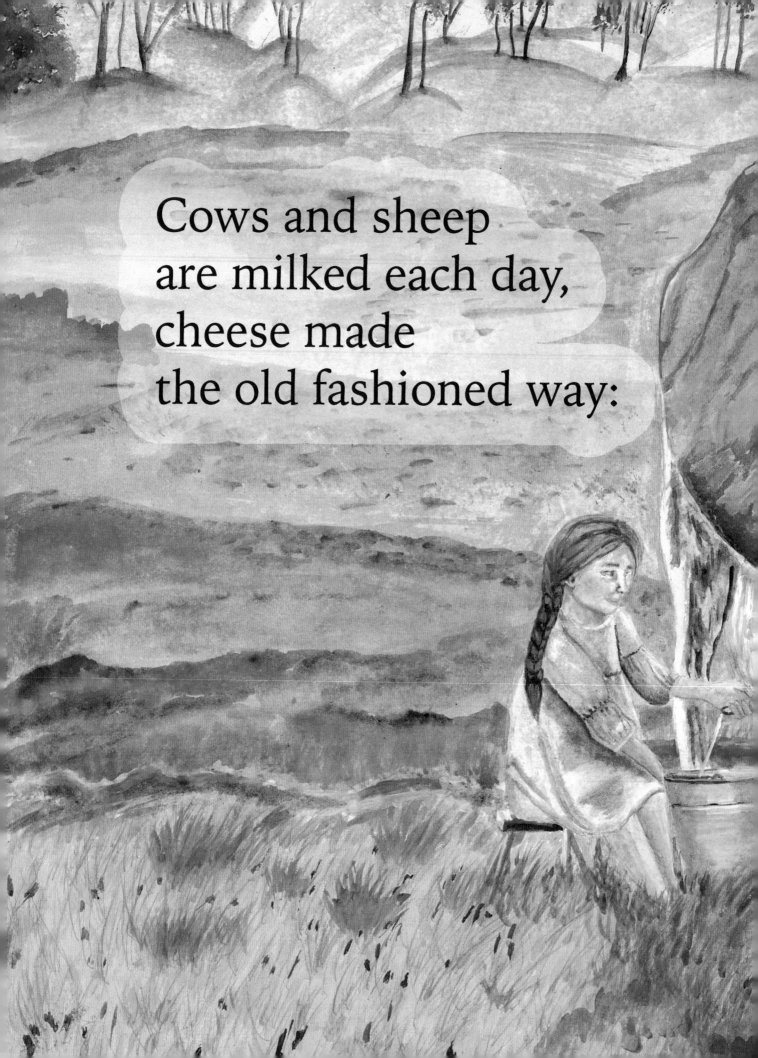

Cows and sheep
are milked each day,
cheese made
the old fashioned way:

In spring
we shear the sheep,

stuff big sacks
with wool to keep,

to knit sweaters
by candle lights,

Children contribute
to the family work:

carrying in wood
and water,

and caring for
a younger brother.

Merry children rush out
of their homes to play,

living life
to the fullest
every day.

Rural Crafts and Farm Activities

The country is linked with farming, agriculture, and occupational skills of the people in the community.

Cabbage

Cabbages are harvested in autumn. They are pickled in saltwater to last through the winter. The result is a delicious and crunchy sour cabbage.

Corn

Corn is harvested in autumn. Corn kernels are scraped off the cobs, fed to animals and birds, like cows, pigs, chickens, or ground into fine cornmeal, which can be made into polenta for human consumption.

Farming with Horses

Horses help to cultivate and harvest the fields, as well as can help with daily tasks on the farm, such as hauling carts.

Hay

Hay is grass which has been cut and dried in the field. It is transported to the farm so that it can be used to feed animals in winter.

Dough

Flour mixed with water, salt, and yeast, and left to rise to double in size, then baked in the oven.

Bread

Bread is prepared from a dough, by baking it in the oven. A baked bread has a deep golden-brown crust and fluffy interior.

Sheepfold

A sheepfold is an enclosure where sheep are penned overnight. Shepherds and dogs watch them at night, to protect them from wolves and bears.

Milking

Removing milk from the mammary glands of an animal, such as cow, goat, or sheep, for human consumption, or to make dairy products, such as cheese, yoghurt, milk cream.

Cheese

Sheep, goat, or cow's milk is warmed-up, fermented with friendly bacteria, until it turns solid or curdle. Cheese is formed in a cheesecloth, which holds solid curds together, as the liquid whey drips out.

Drying the Cheese

Cheese is removed from the cheesecloth to air dry on a cheese stand. The longer a cheese stands, the tastier it becomes. It is called aging.

Sheep Shearing

Sheep's wool can grow too much and sheep get overheated if wool is not removed. The process of cutting the wool off a sheep is called shearing and it is harmless for the sheep.

Wool Spinning

Spinning is the activity of turning wool into yarn, so that it can be further used in knitting, weaving, crocheting clothes and home textiles.

Weaving

Weaving is the craft of lacing fibers together to make fabric or cloth. It involves using a loom to hold the threads, while the weaver throws the filling yarn.

Printed in Great Britain
by Amazon